This Book Is a Gift for

_____

From

_____

MICHAEL A. CAMPION, PH.D.
with photographs by Wilmer Zehr

Bethany Fellowship INC.
MINNEAPOLIS, MINNESOTA 55438

Copyright © 1979
Bethany Fellowship, Inc.
All rights reserved

Published by Bethany Fellowship, Inc.
6820 Auto Club Road
Minneapolis, Minnesota 55438

Printed in the United States of America

ISBN 0-87123-138-7

TO INTRODUCE YOU TO

Especially for Wives

The *Especially for...* series *(Husbands, Parents,* and now *Wives)* is the culmination of years of research and counselling with different people, discovering what they are looking for in inter- personal relationships. Hundreds of women were asked what they wanted in a husband. *Especially for Husbands* was the result. And in the *Especially for Parents* book, children of various ages were surveyed as to what their parents could do to provide a more loving and creative parent-child relationship. "When was the last time..." ques- tions help to put in very practical and everyday form these expectations.

Especially for Wives carries on the tradition. This book was written for women after several hundred men responded to questions concerning their desires for the husband-wife relationship.

This book uses a different approach from the many self-improvement books written by women for women. From the data collected, it becomes clear that men and women *are* different; one or the other is not better, just different. It seems, then, that the essence of marital accord is learning to better understand and cope with these differ- ences in sexual desires, patience, interests, role frustrations, and other areas too numerous to list.

The key to maintaining this accord with one's husband must be found within the context of God's wisdom and love. I Peter 3:4 states, "Be beautiful inside, in your hearts, with the lasting charm of a gentle and quiet spirit which is so pre- cious to God." Women are not born knowing how to be wives; this must be learned. We hope that the ideas presented in *Especially for Wives* will be part of that learning process. So...

when was the last time...

I
Hugged
my
mother-
in-law?

*I had
a good,
open
Conversation
with my
husband?*

I was more aggressive in Sex?

I kept his
his
Favorite
food
in the
refrigerator?

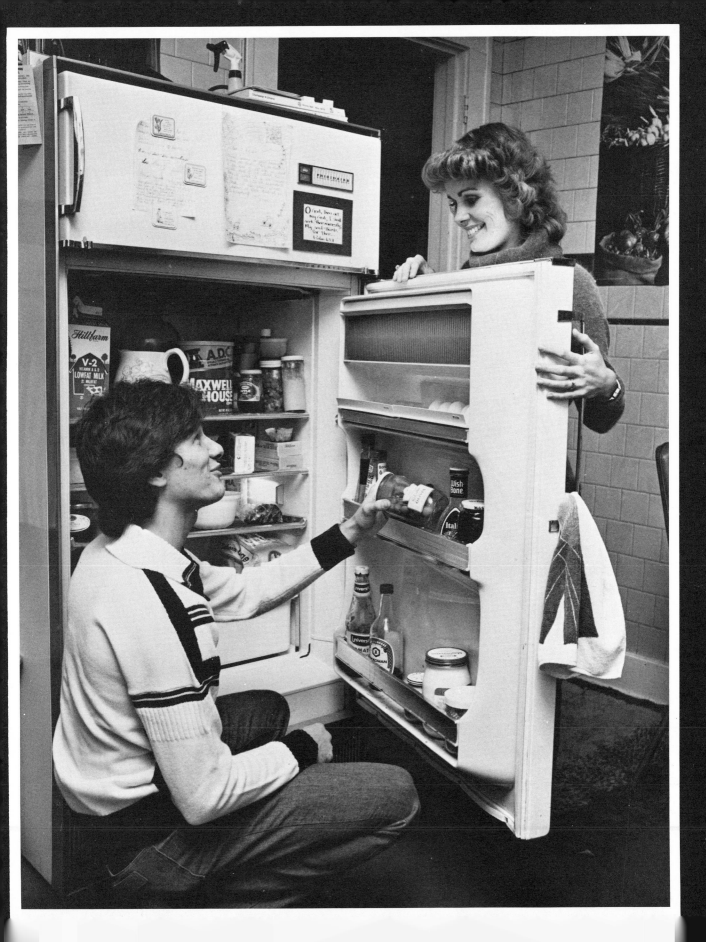

*I
encouraged
the family
to take
a
Vacation
together?*

*I took
up
Activities
or
friendships
outside
our home?*

I was Comfortable with my body?

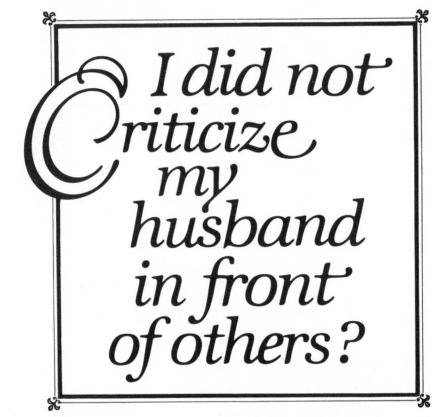

Criticize my husband in front of others?

I did not put my cold Feet in the middle of his back?

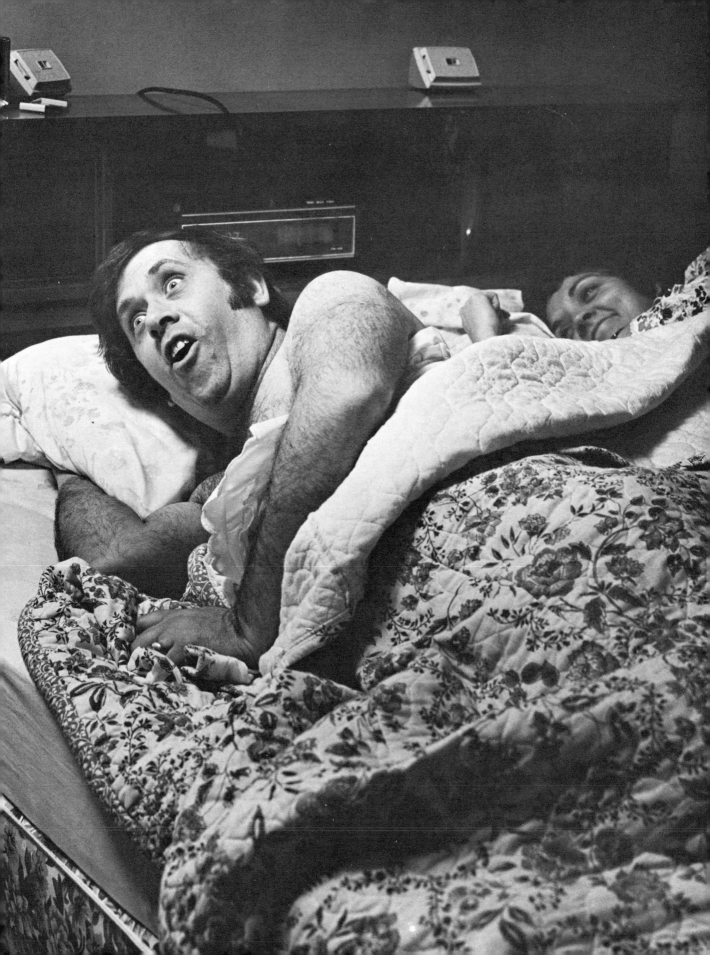

I Supported my husband in the disciplining of our children?

I gave my husband a chance to Express his frustrations when he arrived home from work?

I

Accepted and tried to understand my husband's family?

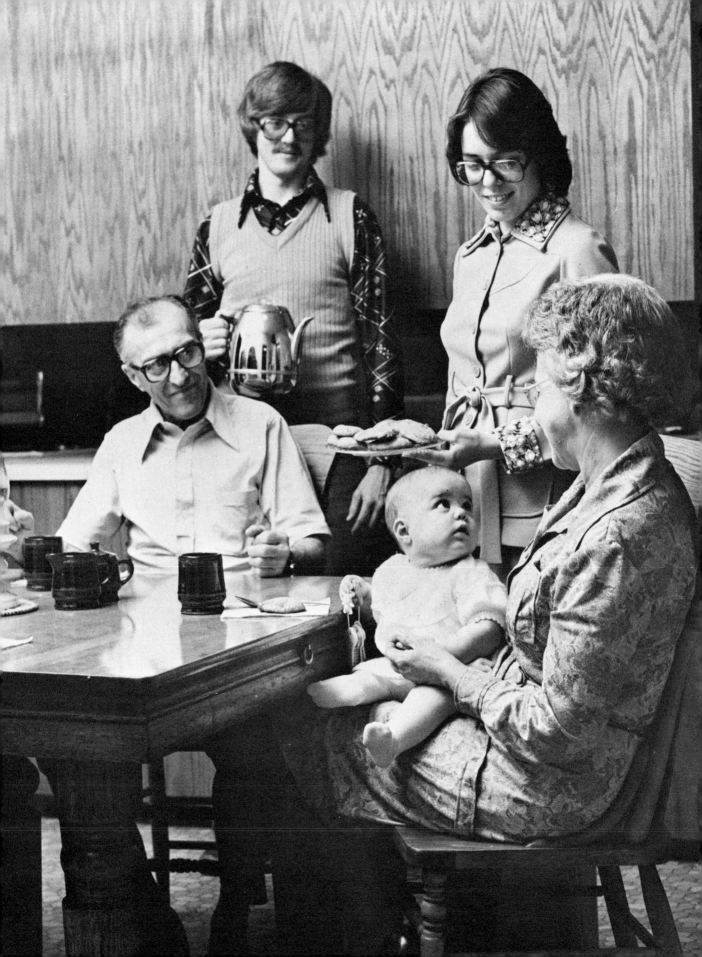

I listened carefully to what he had to say without Pre-judging?

I Cleaned off the top of the refrigerator?

I surprised my husband with an unexpected *Kiss*?

*I placed
my
husband
and
children
before
my
Career?*

I Respected him and let him know it?

I took time for prayer and Bible study with my husband?

I was
passionate
and playful
at Love-
making?

I accepted Criticism graciously?

I showed Enthusiasm for things that are important to him?

I Developed my own interests?

I Slimmed down?

I took Pride in my career?

*I did not
take
all the
Covers?*

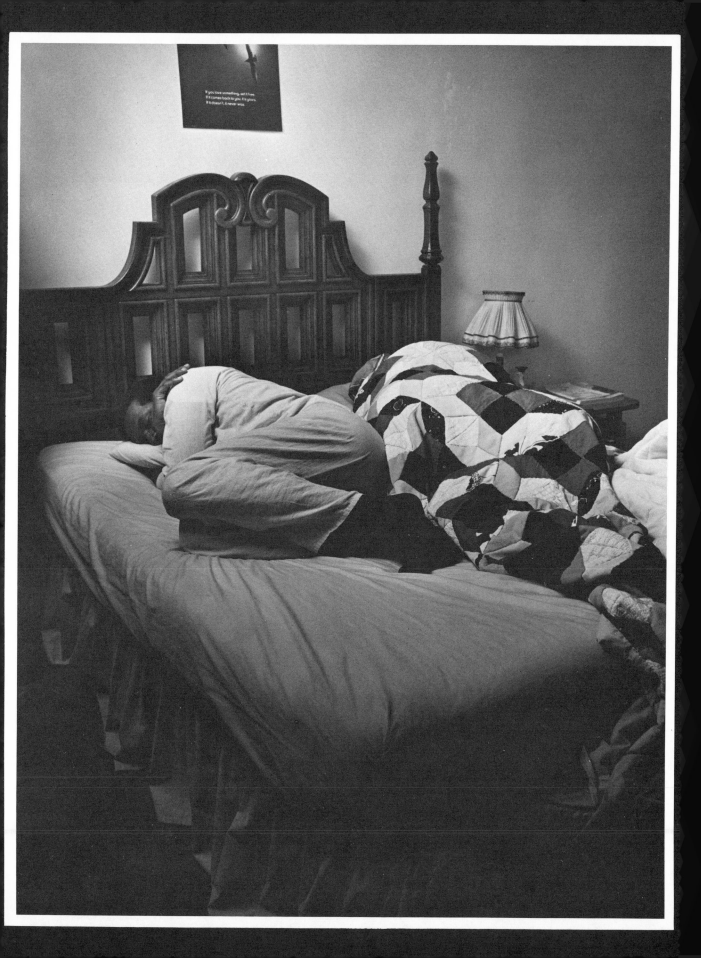

I Loved my husband when he was in a bad mood?

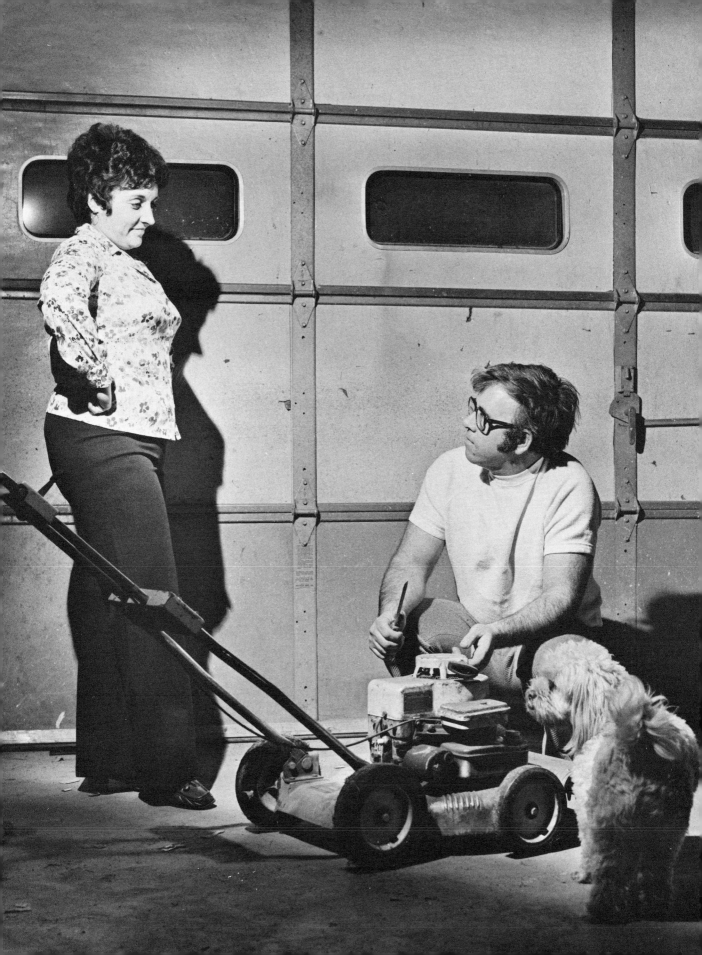

I worked on my own Relationship with God?

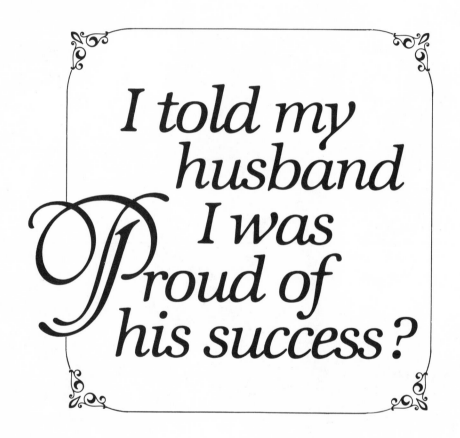

I told my husband I was Proud of his success?

I was
not
Uptight
about
the
housework?

I stopped Talking on the phone when my husband came home from work?

*I talked
rather than
kept silent
when
I was
Upset ?*

I wore Clothes he liked?

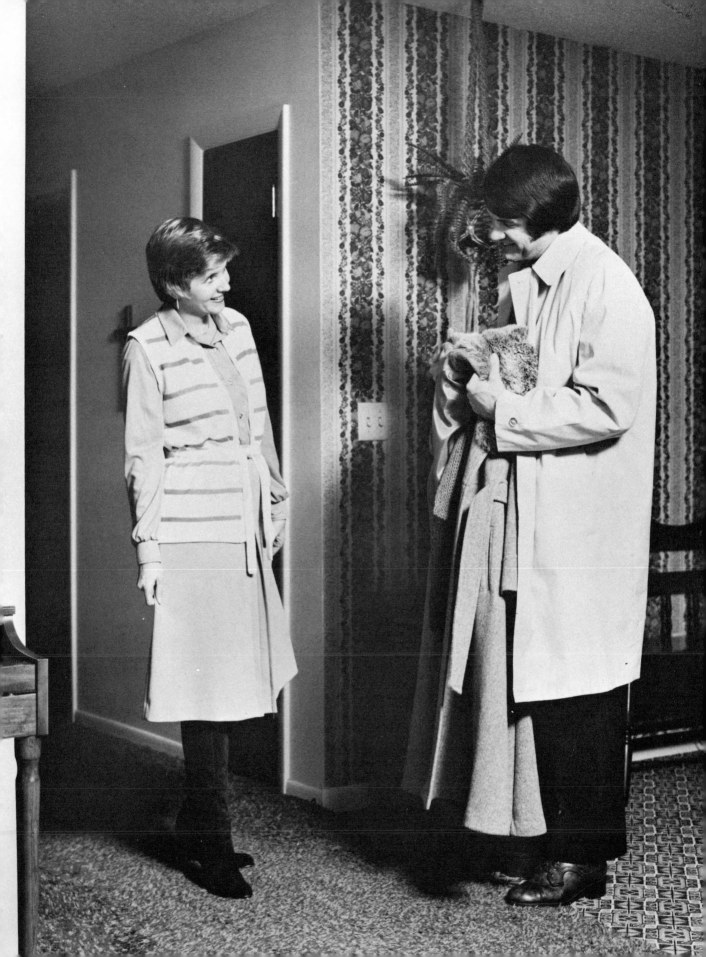

I Smiled when my husband came home from work?

I did
not use
sex as a
Weapon?

*I did not
bring up
his
past
Mistakes?*

I let my husband know before I went out and Bought something?

I was satisfied with my Role as wife and mother?

I was Understanding when he had to work late?

I showed
confidence
in my
husband's
Leadership?

I Accepted disappoint-ment?

*I was
sexually
Relaxed
and
free?*

I did not resent the times my husband was away from *Home* doing other things?

I told my husband I Loved him?

SELF-EVALUATION
FOR WIVES

The following inventory is a self-evaluation of your relationship to your husband. Circle the number in front of the statement which best estimates your frequency of doing that particular behavior. For example: 0, 1, 2, 3, 4, I TOLD HIM I WAS HAPPY WITH HIS SALARY. If you told your husband you were happy with his salary one time in the last twelve months, circle the one.

Respond in like manner to all 50 statements, and then total your score. If some behavior is not applicable to your situation, give yourself a total of 4 points. Have a friend of yours who is married, or several friends that are married, take the inventory and compare your results. For your convenience, you may wish to record your scores below with the date and re-examine yourself yearly or monthly and measure your progress. Now go back over your self-evaluation and pick out one behavior that you would like to do with or for your husband this week and try to do it.

Date and result of self-evaluation:

Date _____ Score_____

Date _____ Score_____

Date _____ Score_____

Date _____ Score_____

Date _____ Score_____

Date _____ Score_____

Date _____ Score_____

SELF-EVALUATION FOR WIVES

Circle Response: TIMES LAST 12 MOS.	Rate yourself. You might wish to compare your score with a friend's.

	When was the last time...
0 1 2 3 4 *(Or More)*	I hugged my mother-in-law?
0 1 2 3 4	I had a good, open coversation with my husband?
0 1 2 3 4	I was more aggressive in sex?
0 1 2 3 4	I prayed for him while he was at work?
0 1 2 3 4	I kept his favorite food in the refrigerator?
0 1 2 3 4	I told him I was happy with his salary?
0 1 2 3 4	I encouraged the family to take a vacation together?
0 1 2 3 4	I kissed my husband when he left for work?
0 1 2 3 4	I took up activities or friendships outside our home?
0 1 2 3 4	I was comfortable with my body?
0 1 2 3 4	I did not criticize my husband in front of others?
0 1 2 3 4	I did not put my cold feet in the middle of his back?
0 1 2 3 4	I supported my husband in the disciplining of our children?
0 1 2 3 4	I gave my husband a chance to express his frustrations when he arrived home from work?
0 1 2 3 4	I accepted and tried to understand my husband's family?
0 1 2 3 4	I listened carefully to what he had to say without pre-judging?
0 1 2 3 4	I cleaned off the top of the refrigerator?
0 1 2 3 4	I surprised my husband with an unexpected kiss?
0 1 2 3 4	I placed my husband and children before my career?
0 1 2 3 4	I respected him and let him know it?
0 1 2 3 4	I took time for prayer and Bible study with my husband?

0 1 2 3 4	I was passionate and playful at love-making?
0 1 2 3 4	I accepted criticism graciously?
0 1 2 3 4	I showed enthusiasm for things that are important to him?
0 1 2 3 4	I cleaned my car?
0 1 2 3 4	I developed my own interests?
0 1 2 3 4	I slimmed down?
0 1 2 3 4	I expressed pleasure in our sex life?
0 1 2 3 4	I took pride in my career?
0 1 2 3 4	I did not take all the covers?
0 1 2 3 4	I loved my husband when he was in a bad mood?
0 1 2 3 4	I worked on my own relationship with God?
0 1 2 3 4	I laughed at my husband's jokes?
0 1 2 3 4	I told my husband I was proud of his success?
0 1 2 3 4	I was not uptight about the housework?
0 1 2 3 4	I stopped talking on the phone when my husband came home from work?
0 1 2 3 4	I talked rather than kept silent when I was upset?
0 1 2 3 4	I wore clothes he liked?
0 1 2 3 4	I smiled when my husband came home from work?
0 1 2 3 4	I did not use sex as a weapon?
0 1 2 3 4	I did not bring up his past mistakes?
0 1 2 3 4	I let my husband know before I went out and bought something?
0 1 2 3 4	I was satisfied with my role as wife and mother?
0 1 2 3 4	I was understanding when he had to work late?
0 1 2 3 4	I showed confidence in my husband's leadership?
0 1 2 3 4	I accepted disappointment?
0 1 2 3 4	I was sexually relaxed and free?
0 1 2 3 4	I did not resent the times my husband was away from home doing other things?
0 1 2 3 4	I massaged his back?
0 1 2 3 4	I told my husband I loved him?

TOTAL